Contents

KT-469-532

Stranger than Fiction from the Arts Council Collection looks at recent art involving narrative, a genre more readily associated with the spoken and written word than with the visual arts. The high-impact visual nature of film and television, where narrative now also thrives, has influenced many artists.

For the most part, the British artists in *Stranger than Fiction* find the rich narratives in their work within their own experiences and personal histories – 'interior is the new exterior,' Sukhdev Sandhu observes in his essay 'Seeming Other People'. They explore their inner selves, not only for personal discovery and catharsis but also so that others can share and understand their backgrounds. Their narratives often convey a Britain in flux, a world that has been deconstructed, reconstructed and reinvented. *Stranger than Fiction* includes one or two stories that are truly fictitious, some that are true yet laced with fiction, and most that are true but that challenge credibility.

Stranger than Fiction has been created by Isobel Johnstone, Curator of the Arts Council Collection, and Ann Jones, its Curator of Projects. I thank them for developing its premise and for writing the texts on the individual works. They have been ably assisted throughout by Isabel Finch.

Sukhdev Sandhu is currently chief film critic for *The Daily Telegraph*. Ruth Borthwick, Director of Literature at the South Bank Centre, invited him to speak in the Voice Box at the Royal Festival Hall in October 2003 about his ground-breaking new book *London Calling: How Black and Asian Writers Imagined a City* (HarperCollins, 2003) and suggested him as the author for this publication. 'Seeming Other People', his essay for *Stranger than Fiction*, provides a tantalising glimpse into the range of social and cultural issues at the heart of *London Calling*. We thank him most warmly for this contribution. It has also been a delight to work with someone so enthusiastically responsive to the Collection.

Our thanks go as well to Adam Brown of 01.02 for his thoughtful design for this catalogue. Its preparation and production have been carried out by Caroline Wetherilt, the Hayward's Art Publisher, with her usual perception and equanimity, and she has been most effectively assisted by James Dalrymple, our Publishing Co-ordinator. The organisation and preparation of the exhibition has involved the co-operation of the full Collection team, including Jill Constantine, Christie Coutin, Frances Munk, Julia Risness and Richard Nesham. Thanks go to them and to the members of the Hayward's technical and transport staff, particularly Ryan Rodgers and Mark King, Imogen Winter and Nick Rogers. The supporting programme of interpretation has been devised by Clare van Loenen, the Hayward's Head of Public Programmes, and Helen Luckett, our Resources Programmer, and includes an informal publication devised in collaboration with Leeds City Art Gallery and Nottingham Castle, which will engage all venues and grow as the exhibition's tour progresses.

It has been a great pleasure connecting again with all the artists in *Stranger than Fiction* in preparation for the exhibition. We would like to thank them unreservedly for making the show possible. Sadly, Donald Rodney is no longer with us, but the kind attention of the executors of his Estate, in particular Diane Simmonds, has been most valuable. We would also like to thank many galleries and friends, including Martin Barlow, Guy Brett, Irene Bradbury at White Cube, Dale McFarland at Frith Street, Nina Øverli at Victoria Miro, Tristram Pye at Anthony Reynolds, and Bea de Souza at The Agency Contemporary Art Ltd.

Stranger than Fiction opened at Leeds City Art Gallery on 23 April 2004 as a collaboration with Nigel Walsh, its Curator of Exhibitions; his help with the planning and preparation of the show has been invaluable. We thank him, as we do all the galleries involved in the tour.

Susan Ferleger Brades
Director, Hayward Gallery

An air-conditioned modern office block in Delhi. Or perhaps Hyderabad. Maybe even Calcutta or Bangalore. It's midnight, a time when one would expect to hear nothing but the sound of a few desultory cleaning staff vacuuming seminar rooms while listening to Celine Dion songs on a transistor radio. Instead, the place is buzzing with the caffeinated chatter of hundreds of recently graduated twenty-somethings. Many of the boys have pricey and not-necessarily fake designer sunglasses resting on their slicked-back hair. The women finger their recently tweezered eyebrows. All are young and peppy, and all sit in tiny cubicles tapping away at their computers and talking through their headsets to strangers who live anywhere from five to ten thousand miles away.

These are the latest recruits to the 'remote processing' revolution that has swept across India during the last 15 years. Over 1,500 companies, employing well over 100,000 people, make up a software industry that has a value of around £5.3bn and is still growing at a rate of 15-20 per cent each year. The call centres themselves, or 'global servicing resources' as they have been dubbed by public relations spokesmen sensitive to the tarnished reputations these institutions have picked up in Europe and North America, are also expanding; 70 new ones appear annually. Companies such as General Electric, AOL or American Express in the United States, and British Airways and British Telecom in the UK, have relocated large parts of their operations to India. Call directory assistance to ask for details about a bar in London and you will as likely as not be speaking to someone in New Delhi.

The men and women in call centres, cordoned off from the limbless beggars and tented families beyond the walls of the industrial-estate compounds behind which they work, are by and large from middle-class backgrounds. The salaries they earn in these cubicles, while low by Western standards (around US $2,600 a year; the American average is ten times higher), are vastly superior to those they could ever hope to earn in any other profession, and are also far in excess of the average Indian salary (c. US $700).

Call centres have been in the news a lot in recent times. Popular tabloids, so long proponents of deregulation and on-yer-bike economics, rail against the loss of British jobs. The writer George Monbiot, meanwhile, sees this economic trend as a case of imperialist

1. George Monbiot, 'The Flight to India', *The Guardian,* 21 October 2003, p. 25

chickens coming home to roost: 'a historical restitution appears to be taking place, as hundreds of thousands of jobs, many of them good ones, flee to the economy we ruined.'[1]

Yet the most fascinating aspect of call centres is the willingness of workers to undergo selfhood regime changes. Individuals are prepared to conceal or transform their identities. This, as all criminals know, requires a good deal of work. Names must be changed. Gitanjali becomes Hazel; Rabindranath is reborn as Sid. Then begins the task of 'accent neutralisation'. The Indians, a number of whom will have Literature BAS or even PHDS, are told that their voices are treacherous and require reconstruction. Coaches teach them to contort their mouths and to twist their tongues to make them sound less regional, more English or American. They even learn how to laugh as white people do, to speak slickly and positively – 'definitely!', 'sure!', 'certainly!', rather than merely 'ok'.

The trainees are voluntary abductees, smiling mutants, happy to be reprogrammed and reconfigured for their new functions. Working evening and night shifts in order to be in synch with Western daytime, they are instructed in the ways of the foreigner: UK and US flags may be hung on the walls; they are shown sitcoms such as *Only Fools and Horses* and *Friends,* in order to teach them foreign sensibilities; they watch international news via Rupert Murdoch's Star TV so that they may engage in 'regular banter' about flash-floods in Yorkshire or baseball scores with their customers. They also take crash courses in geography, history and the monarchy, and modules on British and American social structures. At no point must they let slip that they're Asian, that they're not cash-poor students or struggling single mothers from Burnley.

These call centres haunt me for many reasons. The versions of Britishness they manufacture spells fiscal – and epistemological – crisis for many Britons. They also represent in miniature some of the key currents of modernity: they are examples of what the French social theorist Marc Auge has dubbed 'non-spaces', areas drained of historical or local memory, anonymous terrains designed for trouble-free financial traffic. Raman Roy, Chief Executive of Spectramind, one of India's grandest call centres,

2. Luke Harding,
'Delhi Calling',
The Guardian,
9 March 2001, p. 2

argues that, 'Geography is history. Distance is irrelevant. Where you are physically located is unimportant.'[2]

Yet geography has always been one of the key mechanisms we British use to define who we are. It is meant to root us, to give us vertebration. Geography and nationality have often been closely intertwined. Whatever happened, come rain, shine or prog rock, we were led to believe that we could always take refuge in our Britishness. We, who ruled the waves, who never shall be slaves, were supposed to draw strength from our insularity.

That no longer seems possible. Britain has splintered. In 1999 a Scottish Parliament and Welsh Assembly were established to devolve power from the metropolitan citadel. A belated response to the resentment felt by those millions of voters who chafed against the indignity of being ruled by a Conservative party with almost no mandate north of Yorkshire or west of Gloucestershire, it coincided with a campaign to set up a Parliament of the North and the run-up to an election for a new Mayor of London.

Increasingly too, we British are encouraged (coerced, say some critics) to see ourselves as Europeans. Whether or not the Euro is adopted in the UK in the next few years, it's undeniable that British people have become more Continental in recent decades. We travel to mainland Europe more often thanks to the lure of cut-price airfares. Back at home we don French sports gear, deck out living rooms with Swedish furniture, eat out at tapas bars, and dance ourselves silly to electronic music from Norway (a country we formerly dubbed 'nul-point Norway' due to its poor performances at the Eurovision Song Contest). The very fabric and texture of quotidian life has subtly shifted.

Britain is also permeated by non-European influences. To some extent it always was, the Empire being just one of the forces for internationalism. Now the rate of cultural mixing has accelerated. Globalisation has scant regard for old-fashioned national borders. Transnational capitalism encourages us to define ourselves by what we consume and through our preferred leisure activities. Our identities, particularly in the bigger cities, are shaped by trends, be they sartorial or architectural, which have developed in Barcelona, Tokyo, Jalandhar and Brooklyn. These can be gleaned simply by cantering through a few websites on the Internet, itself a force for diminishing the importance of physical geography.

At the same time, national symbols that were supposed to give us ballast and belonging no longer have the power to instil automatic respect. This is perhaps a knock-on effect of the tendency of intellectuals, following Eric Hobsbawm and Terence Ranger, to regard tradition as 'invented', rather than organic and timeless. Material factors play a part too: the British monarchy is seen by some as a too-generously-funded warren of in-fighting and human dysfunction; the House of Commons, its powers transferred in large part to select committees, Law Lords rulings and Brussels legislation (not least after its failure to represent the public antipathy to the war in Iraq in 2003), is seen as being increasingly irrelevant; even the BBC, the voice of the British nation, has been desacralised in the wake of broadcasting deregulation.

Since 1990 there have been new waves of legal and illegal immigrants coming to the UK from Somalia and Eritrea, Lithuania and the Balkans, Albania and Iraq. Together with the millions of first-, second- and third-generation settlers from the Commonwealth, they have helped to calibrate Britishness in new ways, not least through their tendency to intermarry to a far greater extent than in other, less polycultural European states. No longer can the whiteness or the religious beliefs of the nation be taken for granted. Indeed, according to political commentator Andrew Marr, 'the imperial project and core values, the class system and rules and religion that held the peoples of these islands together have fallen away.'[3] Small wonder, then, that even a friendly outsider such as Bill Bryson, in his best-selling travelogue *Notes from a Small Island*, characterises the country as a creaky, tumbledythump pensioner forever teetering under a pile of tea-towels and hot-water bottles.

The works of art in *Stranger than Fiction*, even though they only infrequently allude to issues of nation and nationhood, are very much the products of the fragmented, jumbled-up post-Britain in which most of the artists live and work. In thrall to the belief, also shared by many film directors, that life beyond the big cities is one bland flatland of identikit, fast-breeder, corporate-coffee-

3. Andrew Marr, *The Day Britain Died*, 2000, Profile, London, p. 57

4. Zygmunt Bauman,
Liquid Modernity, 2000,
Polity Press, Cambridge,
p. 83

chained city centres, a deadening mush of suburbanised,
post-industrial non-spaces, they show scant interest in depicting
landscapes. Geography is in abeyance. Interior is the new exterior.

This should come as no surprise. Ours is a theory-resistant culture
where, in common with many European nations, grand narratives
are in short supply. Politics has given way to an ersatz and simulated
fame economy, as seen by the popularity of such television series
as *I'm A Celebrity Get Me Out of Here!* and *Celebrity Fame Academy*.
Autobiographies, from the victim memoirs produced by Dave Pelzer
to altogether more tricksy, experimental volumes by Dave Eggers,
are of particular appeal to an island race that has traditionally prized
the singular and quirky.

Yet this collective retreat into selfhood proves puzzling. The
dominant mood in the works in *Stranger than Fiction* is one of
loss, trauma, absence, eerie ambiguity. Photograph or video,
drawing or computer montage, everywhere can be found forms of
deconstruction, unsettled subjectivity, barely locatable dread. Most
of the artists steer clear of the arch, splashy modes of expression that
characterise a lot of 1990s' YBA work – Spunk! Blood! Exclamation
marks! – and baulk from the gleeful pick 'n' mix of post-modern
aesthetics. They wade – quizzically, numbly – through the rubble of
what were once fixed lives, concrete social structures. In so doing
they are representative of a contemporary condition that is described
by Zygmunt Bauman in *Liquid Modernity*:

> Identities seem fixed and solid only when seen, in a flash, from outside.
> Whatever solidity they might have when contemplated from the
> inside of one's own biographical experience appears fragile, vulnerable,
> and constantly torn apart by shearing forces which lay bare its fluidity
> and by cross-currents which threaten to rend in pieces and carry away
> any form they might have acquired.[4]

One of those nodes of solidity used to be the family home that, in
the English cultural imagination, is seen as a castle that keeps at
bay the forces of malignity. It's also a womb, a complex matrix of
warmth, nostalgia, arcadian reassurance. Not in the work of these
artists though. Homes have become as vexed, porous and elusive
as the world outside. This is very apparent in Richard Billingham's
photograph, *Untitled* (1994, cat.4), that shows his dad, Ray, on the

verge of falling down. He is red-faced and almost certainly pissed out of his mind. There's comedy here, as pa does his council-house pratfall. But we can't help but notice the wallpaper and curtains and the dowdy carpet. Who is this photographer taking snaps of an enfeebled, working-class old man? Are we being prurient, getting aesthetic kicks from slumming it, in much the same fashion as those *Bumfights* videos in which smirking cameramen cajole tramps and drunken winos into fighting each other?

I don't myself think so. The series from which this photograph is taken shows too much fondness and gentleness. Yet for all its intimacy, and its attempts not to make the father a pitiful object, we can never escape the feeling that Billingham has moved away from this world, and that he is glad to have done so. The same cannot be said of Zarina Bhimji's *Here was Uganda, as if in the vastness of India* (1999-2001, cat.3). An oppressive menace hangs over this house that has seen better days. Children wear starchy shirts and Sunday best-like clothes, evoking a prim Victoriana. They look directly at the camera, but with no special fondness or curiosity. They are defensive, infant patrols.

Mystery suffuses the shot: something has happened here, but we can't work out what precisely. The house is part of a grander story whose plot we can only hazard guesses about. The circles seem like giant bullet holes, or empty speech bubbles. If these bubbles did contain scripts, they would tell of the sad and grievous history of the thousands of Asians who were tortured and expelled from Uganda in the early 1970s at the behest of the dictator General Idi Amin. They would reflect on what it means for those young Ugandan Indians born in England to have been, at some level, doubly displaced, exiled from two continents – Africa and Asia.

Perhaps the most extraordinary work in *Stranger than Fiction*, and certainly the most moving, is Donald Rodney's *In the House of My Father* (1997, cat.18). One of the final pieces he produced before his death of sickle cell anaemia in 1998, it too delves into the relationship between home and ethnicity. On a white pillow, a hand, belonging to the hospitalised artist, is extended; sitting on the palm is a tiny house, crinkled and fragile, looking like a child's stab at origami and held up by small pins. It could be blown away in an instant.

What is Rodney showing us? The house is made out of his own

5. Andrew Salkey, *Come Home, Malcolm Heartland*, 1976, Hutchinson, London, p. 46

skin. I see in the photo an expression of the artist's weakness and resilience; an oblique symbol of the ongoing tussle between Caribbean people and the British 'motherland', one also articulated by the lead character in Andrew Salkey's novel *Come Home, Martin Heartland,* whose departing vision of the UK involves 'a large white door, at an angle of imminent collapse, with the small figure of a black man, standing in front of it and knocking softly, as if the fist he raised were made of a dab of black cloud.'[5] I also see a dream realised – a dream that life amounts to more than nought, that the weak can construct shelters, however temporary, from the ceaseless storm of homelessness, poverty, isolation.

For Sonia Boyce, home is where the heartache is. She's keen to refocus this trope in an explicitly gendered direction. *Mr Close-friend-of-the-family pays a visit whilst everyone else is out* (1985, cat.5), despite its euphemistic title, is an unsettling drawing that depicts some kind of uncle, casually sporting a Christian cross above his beer belly, about to lay his hands on the girl (the artist herself). She stares out at us. Her gaze is ambiguous: there's misery here, a call for help. The family negates as much as it nurtures. Women's selves are all too often damaged and assailed by the depredations of patriarchy.

A similar sentiment emerges in Tracey Emin's *Why I Never Became a Dancer* (1995, cat.9). It begins with a blissed-out evocation of a golden summer from the past in her home town of Margate. Shaky video footage creates an archive of nostalgic reverie, of pre-lapsarian charm. Coffee parlours and Golden Mile deckchairs fade in and out. Emin, in her simple, almost naïve voiceover, recalls that, 'summer was amazing – nothing to do but dream – it was ideal – sex was something simple – you'd go to a pub, have some chips – then sex ... Sex for me had been an adventure, a learning. I was the innocent.'

Not for long. Word gets round that she's easy. The men use her. Wanting to escape, she enters a dance contest, only for the local lads to start yelling 'Slag' at her. Does she have the final laugh? The film ends with her spinning around in a studio, stripped bare of any furnishings or artefacts that might recall the past, to the sound of Sylvester's 'You Make Me Feel (Mighty Real)'. In dance she feels free. In motion she can liberate herself from history. It's an altogether more optimistic sentiment than anything that could be gleaned from *Megatripolis* (1996, cat.16), Seamus Nicolson's photograph of monged, gurning ravers. They look as if they're about to teeter, not into the altered states of consciousness they might have hoped for, or into fluid, Ecstasy-assisted expansive selfhood, but off the stage onto which they have clambered.

The way in which costume may enhance or conceal identity is explored by a number of artists in *Stranger than Fiction*. In *The Last Supper* (1995, cat.1), Faisal Abdu'Allah wittily juxtaposes two images, that of robe-wearing clerics, and of the same people in modern garb. Where formerly they looked like nobles, now they've become a posse of slouching urban gangstas. Jananne Al-Ani, in *Untitled* (1998, cat.2), shows us five women, presumably Muslims, in items of clothing that we take to be traditional. Against Orientalist notions of Muslim women as farouche and recessive, they look straight at the camera, never giving the impression that they are in any way passive; indeed, it's one of them, Al-Ani herself, who is taking the picture. Her second print shows them in 'Western' clothes, in lycra and T-shirts, their hair slung low. Are they migrants? Do they seem more individual now? More like 'us'? What does that question reveal about the way that we frame and contextualise Middle Eastern women?

In Zineb Sedira's *Self Portraits or the Virgin Mary* (2000, cat.19), the robed woman almost merges into whited-out invisibility. Traditional costume seems to render her opaque and silent. Her pose is so stylised as to resemble those often found in moody hipster style mags. She assimilates into nothingness. This tension between revelation and concealment can also be felt in David Medalla's *The Songs of Songs* (1999, cat.15) in which the artist wears three masks in order to draw attention to himself rather than deflect it. Sedira and Medalla offer us iconic images, ones that evoke monumentality or cultural continuity, and deconstruct them so that the timeless becomes temporal, fetishised folk culture comes to seem socially and historically contingent.

Some of the most delightful works in *Stranger than Fiction* are those that aim straight for the funny bone. Lisa Cheung's *I want to be more Chinese* (1997, cat.7) has great fun with 'Chinese Taste', the idea, so common in the eighteenth century, that the East was the repository of all that was refined, proportionate and discretely decorative. William Hogarth scoffed at this notion, and attacked chinoiserie as 'all childish and ridiculous absurdities of temples, dragons, pagodas and the

6. Quoted in *Chinese Homes: Chinese Traditions in English Homes*, 1992, Geffrye Museum, London, p. 6

fantastic fripperies.'[6] Cheung, in her own fashion, revives these charges as she lines up a series of pretty ceramic plates only to have them feature young women stretching their eyes in a parody of the kind of playground taunt directed at Chinese kids by their classmates. The shelf full of plates resembles a coconut shy at a fairground. Cheung is playing at being a spectacle, but the effect this time is to poke fun at those who still harbour old-fashioned assumptions about the essence of the East.

Equally gigglesome – even more so than Gavin Turk's *Oi!* (1998, cat.21) in which the artist, dressed down as a tramp, plays creative havoc with the idea of the artist as celebrity – is *Jetsam* (1995, cat.8) by Alan Currall. It's a straight-to-camera piece, like a particularly batty edition of *Video Nation* or one of Alan Bennett's *Talking Heads*, and features the artist as a sallow-faced extraterrestrial who crash-lands on earth after his spaceship is zapped by home defence forces. Not that that's immediately clear, for the language he uses to describe his wandering seems at first to have been filched wholesale from the lexicon of banal contemporary alienation. 'I decided, um, to be an artist because I'd always been good at drawing.' He attends art school: 'that's good because, um, I get to meet people from all over. It's quite cosmopolitan.'

Soon though, alarm bells begin to ring. 'Um, fortunately we're kind of polymorphous and we can change our shape into whatever we want ... We thought it best to go human because there seemed to be more of them and they're less likely to notice us. Um, I decided to be English because I wasn't very good at the Scottish accent.' Cultural chameleonism isn't always a life-or-death affair; it can be off-the-cuff, spur-of-the-moment. Currall, with his flat voice, his demeanour as deadpan as Buster Keaton's face, and his skinny white frame draped in a Niggas With Attitude T-shirt, comes over as reasonableness itself. Everyone – holiday-maker or immigrant – who has ever travelled abroad has found him- or herself behaving and talking slightly differently. We change form. We become aliens of sorts. This isn't necessarily a source of tragedy.

Currall's film, like many of the works in this show, is shot in a flat, realist mode that is in keeping with the contemporary visual climate. Hollywood blockbusters – for all their huge budgets, celebrity stars and roaring plots – struggle to achieve the iconic status achieved by such grainy, snatched real-time footage as Abraham Zapruder's home movie of the assassination of JFK, the beating of Rodney King by the LAPD, or the abduction of Jamie Bulger. Whether it's the exponential growth of CCTV in work- and public spaces alike, masturbation fodder in the form of JennicAM and a million on-line voyeur sites, or the popularity of digicam and webcams and phone cameras – the reality effect, or at least, a reality effect, is more sought after than ever before.

'Keep it real', runs the hip-hop mantra that has percolated through urban cultures the world over: 'tell it like it is'. 'Reality' programmes (however confected) pock the television schedules, as do mockumentary comedies such as *The Office* and *I'm Alan Partridge*. Meanwhile, documentary films are doing better business than they have for many years. The Dogme movement in Denmark, kick started by Lars Von Trier and Thomas Vinterberg, enjoined film directors to sign a 'Vow of Chastity' that forbade artificially dramatic devices such as flashbacks, filters and artificial lighting, and mandated the use of handheld cameras.

This relentless assertion of truth, reality and bare-boned verisimilitude is an expression of fear, an attempt to ward off the encroachment of fakeness which can be created more easily than ever before. Simulation, ludic or otherwise, is everywhere for sale: the resurgence of interest in eighteenth-century forger Thomas Chatterton, the computer-generated imagery of Hollywood films such as *Gladiator*, in which the huge crowd scenes are pixellated, makeover series such as *Faking It*. Genetic cloning is commonplace; advanced digital technology has made morphing techniques widely available; the politics of spin and mendacity have been so refined that fabricated 'Weapons of Mass Destruction' are used as a justification for war in the Middle East. Who and what can be trusted?

This is the niggling question that runs through Kenny Macleod's short film *Robbie Fraser* (1998, cat.14). The artist, looking like a King's Cross rent boy or a baby-faced trainee striker at a middling Premier League football team, recites a series of micro-memoirs. All of them begin: 'Hello, my name is Robbie Fraser.' He claims to be 28 and to have moved to London from Aberdeen. Each video entry is shot straight to camera, and delivered in the same apparently guileless Scottish voice. Yet each entry is also slightly different. Details are added and subtracted: he talks about his boyfriend, but later about his girlfriend. He seems to be having a great time, and then later to be in throes of depression. The frayed narrative threads resist being tied up. The more he insists on being Robbie Fraser, the less transparent he becomes. Repetition and minimalism create a more diffuse story.

The film is funny and deeply haunting. 'Robbie Fraser' becomes ever more blank, ever more fugitive. He slips away from us. 'I'm making the best I can out of what I've got,' he says at one point. But what has he got? Is it merely a drive towards being protean, multiple and contradictory? Is this apparent inability to be centred caused by the discombobulating dynamics of capitalism and urban society? Towards the end of the film, 'Robbie' compares his life with that of his mother and father, 'Our experiences are different and cause conflict. Their lives centre on family, mundane work and close-knit family. Here I am in London, still single, and 28, and doing nothing which they would call a profession.'

Robbie's dilemma is shared, however differently inflected, by the rest of the artists in *Stranger than Fiction*. As the sons and daughters of deconstruction, they distrust the old verities – home, nation, history, narrative – which they feel have been used to cover up or foment a multitude of sins. They struggle instead to find new modes of belonging, ports of call in the choppy turbulence of a post-national global order. The truths they search for are elusive. They themselves are too ironic to believe in simple transcriptions of the world around them. Captives of an era in which the portfolio, pluriform self is sovereign – 'A New You For 2004!' – they no longer have a reassuring bedrock of selfhood on which to fall back.

The art that emerges from this strandedness is fascinating, but it's also painful and messy. It leaves me wondering though about those men and women back in Hyderabad. I used to think that what they were doing was outlandish. It turns out though that their interest in switching identities is now the rule rather than the exception. The only difference is that they seem to do this uncomplicatedly, in order to get paid. They have seen the future, and to them it is one of opportunities and promise. By contrast, the artists in *Stranger than Fiction* are still knee-deep in the slurry and confusion of the present.

Plates

Isobel Johnstone
Ann Jones

1. *The Last Supper,*
1995
computer-generated
bromide prints
with selenium
split tone; 2 parts,
each 123 × 180 cm
Purchased from
The Agency, 2001

Born of Jamaican descent in London in 1969, Faisal Abdu'Allah graduated from the Royal College of Art in 1993 with an MA in Fine Art Printmaking, having previously studied at Central St Martins School of Art, London (1988-91) and Massachusetts College of Art, Boston (1989). He shows regularly at The Agency in London and has had recent solo shows at Chisenhale, London (2003) and Aspex Gallery, Portsmouth (2003). Earlier shows include *Heads of State*, Standpoint Gallery, London (1997-98) and *Eyes without a Face*, LKW (1999). Group exhibitions include *Ecce Homo*, Kunsthal, Rotterdam (2000), *B.I.G.,* Torino Biennale, Turin (2002) and *Veil*, an InIVA touring exhibition (2003-04). He lives and works in London.

In *The Last Supper* Faisal Abdu'Allah re-casts white Western versions of a blond, blue-eyed Jesus and the traditional Last Supper scene by presenting different, even conflicting views using black friends and actors. In the first image, men and women are photographed in African-Muslim clothes, a reflection of Abdu'Allah's commitment to the Nation of Islam (a black nationalist re-configuration of traditional Islamic beliefs) and his views on a specifically Nubian religious identity. Judas, a pivotal element in the diptych, stands on the viewer's side of the table facing inwards, a gun held behind his back. The gun is a recurrent motif in Abdu'Allah's work. The artist believes that guns have been romanticised in the media, films and television, while young black men in inner cities are discovering the all too real and tragic outcome of gun-usage. The second image portrays a contemporary group of young people, who stare outwards, challenging the viewer to acknowledge their presence. IJ

All quotes are taken from the Arts Council Collection archives, unless stated otherwise.

2. *Untitled*, 1998
c-type photographs;
2 parts, each
122 × 122 cm
Purchased from
the artist, 2001

Jananne Al-Ani was born in Kirkuk, Iraq in 1966. She studied at the Byam Shaw School of Art, London (1986-89), University of Westminster, London (1991-95) and Royal College of Art, London (1995-97). She has recently had solo shows at the Imperial War Museum, London (1999), Smithsonian Institution, Washington DC (1999) and *Les Rencontres Internationales de la Photographie*, Arles (2002). She also co-curated the InIVA touring exhibition *Veil* in 2003-04. She lives and works in London.

Born in Iraq to an Arab father and Irish mother, much of Jananne Al-Ani's work has been concerned with representation and constructed identities. She became aware of the resilience of Orientalist thinking in the Western consciousness around the time of the outbreak of war in the Gulf in 1991 and, as she says, 'the issues at the heart of the relationship between East and West are the ones that interest me and inform my work.' The five women in the diptych *Untitled* are the artist, her mother and three sisters, shown in both 'Eastern' and 'Western' clothing. Al-Ani has spent a number of years researching representations of Middle Eastern women by late-nineteenth- and early-twentieth-century European photographers. A particular interest of hers has been the studio portrait. The crux of this is her investigation into the role of the camera as a tool of control, the relationship between the gaze of the photographer and the returned gaze of the subjects, and the continuing fascination with these portraits despite the cultural and political shifts that have occurred in the intervening years. AJ

Jananne Al-Ani

3. *Here was Uganda, as if in the vastness of India*, **1999-2001**
cibachrome on aluminium;
122.4 × 172.4 cm
Purchased from Norwich Gallery, 2001

Born in Mbarara, Uganda in 1963 to a family of Indian immigrants, Zarina Bhimji moved to Britain in 1974. She studied at Leicester Polytechnic (1982-83), Goldsmiths College (1983-86) and the Slade School of Fine Art (1988-89). Solo exhibitions include *I will always be here*, Ikon, Birmingham (1992) and shows at Kettles Yard, Cambridge (1995) and Talwar Gallery, New York (2001). Group exhibitions include *Documenta 11*, Kassel, Germany (2001). She lives and works in London.

'In August 1974, two years after Amin's decree, my sister and I had to suddenly flee leaving behind everything except two dresses and a cardigan. Due to the circumstance we had been in hiding in a small village, Ntungamo. We stayed indoors with curtains closed. I witnessed violence, shooting and death by Amin's military. In the summer of 1998 I visited Uganda for the first time in 24 years. I visited many places that suffered badly during the civil war.'

This personal account of Bhimji's return to Uganda after the atrocities of civil war alludes to the background and inspiration for a large new body of her work. In this photograph and others, as well as in film, Bhimji researches the physical evidence left on buildings, airports, graveyards, military barracks and police cells of a reign of terror that shattered many lives. Up to this point in her career her work had involved fragile and tentative accumulation, invariably photographically based, of evidence and fragments relating to the body and feminine identity. By contrast, this new work is spare with minimal artistic intervention. It is an elegy to a double diaspora, and one that is created without the representation of personal history. IJ

4. *Untitled*, 1994
SFA4 colour
photograph on
aluminium;
105 × 158 cm
Purchased from
Anthony Reynolds
Gallery, 1997

Richard Billingham
was born in
Birmingham in 1970.
He graduated from
the University of
Sunderland in 1994.
He was awarded
the first Citibank
Photography Prize in
1997 and was short-
listed for the Turner
Prize in 2001. He has
had solo exhibitions
at the National
Museum of Film
and Photography,
Bradford (1996),
British School at
Rome (1999) and
Ikon Gallery,
Birmingham (2000),
as well as regular
exhibitions at
Anthony Reynolds
Gallery, London.
He now lives and
works in Stourbridge.

This is a portrait of the artist's father, Ray, and is one of a series of photographs of Billingham's parents, brother and pets in their West Midlands flat. Billingham has explained that his father is a chronic alcoholic and that his mother, Liz, left due to Ray's incessant drinking and moaning. Billingham began to take these photographs in the early 1990s as reference material for his paintings. He then realised that through the photographs he could look at his family 'from the outside, in a different light', and in the process he could understand both them and himself more fully. In 1996 he published the photographs in a book entitled *Ray's a Laugh* (Scalo, Zurich). The photographs of this tragi-comedy of domestic life are poignant and startlingly direct. Billingham writes about this series of photographs, 'I never wanted to shock people with my work. I wanted to surprise them, perhaps, but not to shock them. I wanted the book to be like a play that moves the viewer.' AJ

(First published in *Here to Stay*, 1998, exhibition catalogue, Hayward Gallery Publishing, London, p. 18)

Richard Billingham

5. *Mr Close-friend-of-
    the-family pays
    a visit whilst everyone
    else is out*, 1985
    charcoal on paper;
    109.2 × 150 cm
    Purchased from the
    artist, 1989

Born in London in 1962, Sonia Boyce is one of five children; her mother was from Barbados and her father from Guyana. She studied at Stourbridge College of Art and Technology (1980-83). From 1996 until 2002 she co-directed AAVAA (African and Asian Visual Artists Archive) with David A. Bailey at University of East London. Solo exhibitions include *Sonia Boyce*, AIR Gallery, London (1986-87), *Peep*, Brighton Museum and Art Gallery and InIVA (1995), *Sonia Boyce: Performance*, Cornerhouse, Manchester (1998) and *Recent Sonia Boyce: La, La, La*, Douglas F. Cooley Memorial Art Gallery, Reed College, Portland (2001). Group shows include *The Other Story: Afro-Asian Art in Post-war Britain*, Hayward Gallery, London (1989), *Mirage: Enigmas of Race, Difference and Desire*, ICA, London (1995), and *Century City*, Tate Modern, London (2001). Sonia Boyce lives and works in London.

Sonia Boyce's practice is wide-ranging and includes painting, collage, photography, installation and, recently, working collaboratively with singers. In the mid-1980s she was known for her pastel drawings. When she was a student, her black contemporaries, Keith Piper and Eddie Chambers, set a tough political agenda but she found her own means of expression through personal experience and the inspirational examples of Frida Kahlo and women artist friends like Claudette Johnson and Lubaina Himid. After leaving college in 1983, she began a series of portraits of herself and members of her family. Often incorporating patterns, these large coloured pastels carry ironical texts enhancing her instructive story of an Afro-Caribbean woman growing up in what was still a fairly hostile Britain. The feminine agenda was high at this time. In this stark black-and-white work, a faceless 'Mr Close-friend-of-the-family' reaches towards the artist who looks out in alarm, appealing to the viewer. A domestic background of leafy wallpaper becomes a frame of groping hands, threatening to cling to the artist like seaweed. IJ

6. *No One Can Tell*, 1993
photograph; 2 parts,
each 299 × 183 cm
Purchased from
Anthony Reynolds
Gallery, 1999

Born in Derby in 1943, Ian Breakwell studied at Derby College of Art (1960-64) and at West of England College, Bristol (1965). His practice includes painting, printmaking, performance, photography, video and film. Solo shows include *Continuous Diary 1965-1978*, Third Eye Centre, Glasgow (1978), *The Waiting Room*, Matt's Gallery, London (1985), *Self Portraits*, Anthony Reynolds Gallery, London (1986), *Double Life, two installations*, PICA, Perth, Australia (1990), *Mask to Mask*, Oriel and Ffotogallery, Cardiff (1993) and *Death's Dance Floor*, Ffotogallery, Cardiff (1998) and Streetlevel, Glasgow (1999). He shows regularly at Anthony Reynolds Gallery in London, the city where he lives and works.

This double photograph evolved from a series about twins and is part of Ian Breakwell's study of the human face and the mask. Twins fascinate the artist because of their telepathic kinship, representing, as he says, 'a potential for heightened communication, which has become blunted and diluted in everyday life for us non-twins. If we retained the uninhibited reactions of the child we would be a source of perpetual embarrassment, so we all wear masks and tacitly agree to abide by social conventions of behaviour.' *Twin Audience*, which was the principal work in the exhibition *Mask to Mask* at Oriel and Ffotogallery, Cardiff (1993), involved the filming and photography by David Daggers of 40 pairs of twins. They were asked to respond to demands such as 'Imagine you have just had a great shock' and most of them reacted with surprising synchronicity. Among these twins were William and Jim Edwards from Pontardawe, Wales, who appear together life-sized in *No One Can Tell*. Separated from their mother at birth because of pleurisy, the artist recalls that this most affectionate pair was the closest of all 40 twins – they were 'incubated in a bread oven' and are 'very moving wonderful people' [Ian Breakwell, from a conversation with Martin Barlow when *No One Can Tell* was shown in the *Intimacy* exhibition at the Oriel Mostyn, Llandudno, 2001]. In one part of the work, one twin covers the mouth of the other with his hand and, in the other, the other does so – or is it the same twin silencing the other each time? No one can tell... IJ

Ian Breakwell

7. *I Want to be More Chinese*, 1997
photo-emulsion on ceramic; 10 parts, maximum 25 cm diameter
Purchased from Whitechapel Art Gallery, 1998

Born in Hong Kong in 1969, Lisa Cheung was brought up in Canada. She studied Fine Arts at Queens University, Kingston, Ontario (1989-92) and at Goldsmiths College, London (1996-98). Projects, residencies and exhibitions include *Gracelands Palace*, Sungkok Museum, Seoul (1999), *How the West was Lost and Won*, British Council Windows Gallery, Prague (2000), *New Year*, Chinese Arts Centre, Manchester (2000), *Tea Set*, Derby Museum and Art Gallery (2002), *Twilight Gardens*, Camden Arts Centre, London (2001-02), *Art and Food*, Victoria and Albert Museum, London (2003), *Carioquinha*, Espaco Bananeias, Rio de Janeiro (2003) and *Did you know that Hong Kong was still last night?*, Para/Site Art Space, Hong Kong (2003). Lisa Cheung works and lives and in London.

Participation is now a frequent element in Lisa Cheung's art practice, which involves working in a wide range of ways, with light, multiples and environments. The materials used in these interactive inventions are simple and as diverse as vegetables, sweets, paper and fairy lights. *I Want to be More Chinese* was made during her studies at Goldsmiths College in 1996-98 and was shown in The Whitechapel Open. It is one half of a series of 20 china plates made with the co-operation of friends, who posed to have their photographs taken so that the images could be transferred onto found plates. This work is a play on how we see ourselves and how we are perceived by others. Here, the artist celebrates her identity, subverting a negative gesture of difference by asserting her desire to be more so. Her playful approach, which materialises in decorative and colourful installations, is motivated by the serious aim of encouraging people to appreciate their own and others' creativity. IJ

Lisa Cheung

8. *Jetsam*, 1995 (still)
Betacam sp video
tape with sound;
running time:
3 minutes, 47 seconds
Purchased from the
artist, 1997

Alan Currall was born in Stoke-on-Trent in 1964. He studied at Stafford University (1989-92) and Glasgow School of Art (1994-95). He has had solo shows at the Australia Centre for Contemporary Art, Melbourne (2000), Stills Gallery, Edinburgh (2001) and Jerwood Space, London (2002). He was included in *New Contemporaries* in 1996 and in *Becks Futures* in 2003. He lives and works in Glasgow.

Jetsam is concerned with identity and also with Currall's own personal crisis when he found himself, once again, 'out in the "real" world' after graduating from Glasgow School of Art. As a metaphor for this, he recounts in this monologue a fantastical tale of being an alien who has just crash-landed in Scotland. It is all relayed in a deadpan manner, as Currall sits facing the camera in a position reminiscent of television broadcasts of hostages. As the humorous story unfolds, we learn how he has morphed into a human as 'there seemed to be more of them', and how he has decided to be English as he isn't very good at a Scottish accent. He works one day a week at an art school, as he's always been good at drawing. The narrative skilfully interweaves the bizarre with the poignant as he relays that the other aliens he arrived with also have jobs, though one is on the dole, and concludes by confiding, 'I miss home [...] Quite a good job I've got really, flying saucers.' AJ

9. *Why I Never Became a Dancer*, 1995 (still)
Betacam sp video tape on monitor or projected with sound; running time: 6 minutes, 40 seconds
Purchased from White Cube, 1998

Tracey Emin was born in London in 1963, but grew up in Margate. She studied at the Maidstone College of Art (1983-86) and Royal College of Art, London (1987-89). She has exhibited regularly at White Cube, London and has had solo exhibitions at the South London Art Gallery (1997), Modern Art Oxford (2002), Stedelijk Museum, Amsterdam (2002) and Art Gallery of New South Wales, Australia (2003). She was short-listed for the Turner Prize in 1999. She lives and works in London.

Tracey Emin

Tracey Emin has used her own life story as the prime source material for her work. Using texts, embroidery, video, installation, drawing and painting, she relates, in a direct and moving manner, the tragedies and poignant and humorous moments that have befallen her.

Why I Never Became a Dancer is likewise autobiographical. Here she recalls her teenage bid to leave the seaside town of Margate, where she grew up, by entering the British Disco Dancing Championship of 1978. However, as she danced, she was humiliated by a group of boys chanting, 'Slag, Slag, Slag'. In the video, her final words are, 'Shane, Eddy, Tony, Doug, Richard. This one's for you,' as she gains her freedom and dances away from the small-town world. She recalls, 'As a 15-year-old girl I had outgrown not just my home town, but also the men in it. I'm NOT A SLAG, I just loved sex, that's all.' AJ

10. *Humayan's Tomb
from the series
Exiles*, 1987
c-type print;
48.2 × 48.2 cm
Purchased from the
artist, 1988

Sunil Gupta was born in New Delhi, India in 1953. He studied at Concordia University, Montreal (1972–77), West Surrey College of Art, Farnham (1978–81) and the Royal College of Art, London (1981–83). A founder member of Autograph (The Association of Black Photographers), Gupta is also a writer and curator. He has had solo exhibitions at the Contemporary Art Gallery, Vancouver (1994), Portfolio, Edinburgh (1997), John Hansard Gallery, Southampton (2003), City Art Gallery, Leicester (2004) and California Museum of Photography, Riverside, California (2004). A Canadian citizen, he currently lives and works in London.

In 1987, the fortieth year of Indian independence, Sunil Gupta wrote that the year also marked 'the continued suppression of gay men. Sexuality is not on the development agenda [...] The gains made by gay activists in the West to foster a positive gay identity and culture filter in, but obviously their tactics cannot be exactly duplicated in India. On the other hand, AIDS has arrived to reinforce all the worst stereotypes [...] Without cultural expression, and with the complexities of a large multi-lingual country, deeply divided by caste and class, and the sharp contrast between rural and urban, the homosexual community lacks a national identity. The work presented here is a review of this particular situation. It is located in Delhi, the capital of successive empires, around the sites where gay men meet. The participants are all gay men who agree that although there is difficulty in formulating a public demand for their rights, a discussion might begin in the cultural arena. Male homosexual activity remains illegal, a hangover of the Raj conveniently left untouched in the ardent drive to Sanskritise the nation.' [Sunil Gupta, 1987, quoted in *Shocks to the System*, 1991, exhibition catalogue, National Touring Exhibitions, South Bank Centre, London, p. 46]

Sunil Gupta

11. *Airline No.2*, 1990
black-and-white
photograph and LEDs;
117 × 178 cm
Gift of Charles Saatchi,
1999

Graham Gussin was born in London in 1960. He studied at Middlesex Polytechnic (1981-85) and Chelsea College of Art, London (1989-90). He has recently had solo exhibitions at Tate Britain, London (*Art Now*, 1998), Kunsthalle Aarhus , Denmark (1999), Ikon, Birmingham (2002) and Lisson Gallery, London (2003). He was also included in the Henry Moore Foundation exhibition at the Venice Biennale in 2003. He lives and works in London.

A silhouetted image of a family gathered in anticipation of an unexplained event or happening occupies the foreground in the vast and stunning landscape in *Airline No.2*. Gussin re-photographed the image from a book of photographs of American landscapes taken just after the Second World War called *Our Beautiful Land*. While the publication was partly funded by the Farm and Land Survey and was presented as a documentary study, many of the photos are highly romanticised images. The red LED lights scattered across the surface of Gussin's work represent airports from around the world, perhaps emphasising a sense of scale. Gussin has noted, 'they are really points of arrival or departure. I was interested in these two senses of place coming together, colliding perhaps. The lights become a graffiti across the surface.' AJ

Graham Gussin

Mount Hood   *Ray Atkeson*

12. *Star*, 1994 (still)
black-and-white Super-8
film with sound;
running time: 3 minutes
Purchased from Frith
Street Gallery, 1997

Born in Dublin in 1966, Jaki Irvine completed her sculpture studies at the National College of Art and Design in 1989 and then her MA in Fine Art at Goldsmiths College, London in 1994. Solo exhibitions include shows at Frith Street Gallery, London (1997 and 2000) and Kerlin Gallery, Dublin (2004). Group exhibitions include *White Noise*, Kunsthalle, Bern (1998), *New British Art 2000: Intelligence*, Tate Britain, London (2000), *Video in the City*, Venice Biennale (2001) and *Art Now – Lightbox*, Tate Britain, London (2003).

Casually observed conversations and encounters are often the starting point and, ostensibly, the content of Jaki Irvine's work. But she chooses visual effects, scripts and music that confound, rather than construct, a coherent narrative, believing that such complexity is closer to real life. She has commented on her interest in exploring, '...those points where what at first seems most available to understanding, slowly turns opaque, revealing itself as misleading or meaningless. If this then opens out a sense of untold distances between things, and people, it also brings with it a desire for the reverse, gesturing towards impossibly compensatory intimacies between ourselves and the world [...] towards a belief in the transparency and agreement of things – of gestures, smiles, meanings, chance remarks and strangers.' [Jaki Irvine, *New British Art 2000: Intelligence*, 2000, exhibition catalogue, Tate, p. 70] IJ

Excerpt from *Star*, 1994

This is a dry story with a lot of Vodka

Two people, a man and a woman,
meet each other in a pub.
They enter and then they sit down.

But,
they don't sit down close to each other,
they just take their place on the opposite
side of the bar.

And then the woman is shouting to the man

Hey handicap
would you like to have another vodka?

Hey, handicap,
would you like to have another vodka?

Hey handicap,
would you like another vodka?

And she asks this several times

And after a while and she has drunken a lot
She fell down on the floor
like a star.

Text: Jaki Irvine
Voice: Anke Dessin
Music: Sergei Prokofiev,
'Waltz of the Diamonds'

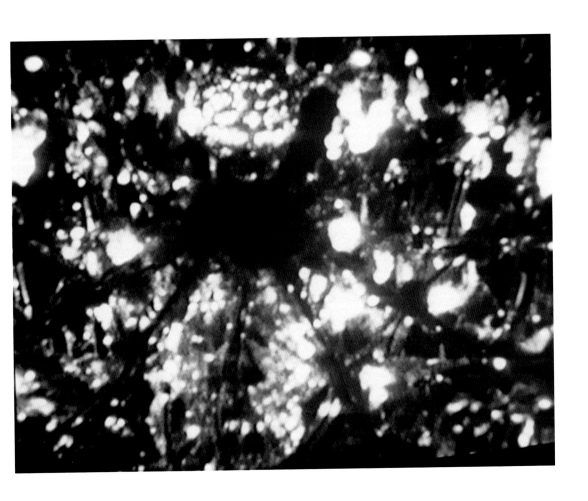

13. *The Long Road to Mazatlan*, **1999 (still)**
Collaboration:
Isaac Julien and
Javier de Frutos
Director: Isaac Julien
Choreography and
movement:
Javier de Frutos

video projection on
DVD with sound;
running time:
20 minutes
Purchased from
Victoria Miro Gallery,
2001

Born in London in 1960, Isaac Julien studied at Central St Martins School of Art, London (1980-84). Initially a painter, he was soon immersed in film, working as a writer, director, even on occasion as an actor. He is also an influential theorist and teacher. He explores identity, desire and history and challenges divisions between artistic disciplines. After *Looking for Langston* (1989), a poetic documentary-biography of the Harlem Renaissance poet Langston Hughes, he began to create multi-channel works for gallery viewing. Recent examples include *Vagabondia* (2000) and *Paradise/ Omeros* (2002). Group shows include *Rhapsodies in Black: Art of the Harlem Renaissance*, Hayward Gallery, London (1997) and *Tate Turner Prize*, Tate Britain, London (2001). He shows at Victoria Miro Gallery in London, the city where he lives and works.

There are two protagonists in *The Long Road to Mazatlan* – cowboys dressed in classic contrast, one in a white top, jeans and a hat, the other in a dark outfit. One is Javier de Frutos, a London-based dancer and choreographer; the other is Phillippe Riera. The film explores the myth of the cowboy, the outcast and the pioneer, ideas all too familiar to Isaac Julien from personal experience and a store of cinematic memories, such as James Dean walking away in *Giant* and Andy Walhol's film *Cowboys*.

The act of looking is intrinsic to this film, which is full of seductive colour, for example, in the sparkling swimming pool sequences that recall David Hockney paintings. The title is taken from Tennessee Williams' play *The Night of the Iguana* and signifies the end of the road. As the film closes the two men perform a jerky road-side dance – 'movements of repression,' says Julien, '...of discombobulated desire', a glimpse of how desire surfaces when it is unmediated and not inspired by a role we recognise from films or books. 'It's the stereotype we find engaging,' says Julien. 'We depend on it. We're not always undone by stereotypes – in some ways they sustain us.' [David Frankel in conversation with Isaac Julien, December 1999] IJ

Isaac Julien

14. *Robbie Fraser*, 1998
(still)
Betacam sp video
tape with sound;
running time:
17 minutes
Purchased from the
artist, 1999

Born in Aberdeen in 1967, Kenny Macleod studied at Goldsmiths College, London (1996-99) and at the Rijksakademie van beeldende kunsten, Amsterdam (2000-02). Recent exhibitions include shows at the Musée d'Art Contemporain, Lyon (2002), Stedelijk Museum Bureau, Amsterdam (2002), Apex Art, New York (2002), Lokaal 01, Antwerp (2002), Herzliya Museum of Art, Israel (2001), Poëziezomer Watou, Belgium (2001), Frankfurter Kunstverein (2001) and *Black Box Recorder*, British Council International Touring Exhibition (2000), *The British Art Show 5*, National Touring Exhibitions, Hayward Gallery, London (2000) and *New Contemporaries*, Liverpool (1999). Kenny Macleod lives and works in Amsterdam.

'The work started quite abstractly – I decided on a sequence of exactly 100 word narrative texts, each beginning with the same sentence – "Hello, my name is Robbie Fraser" – and *then* I filled in the details. If the details of the stories did not fit 100 words, they were pruned or padded rigorously so they fitted exactly. It didn't matter whether what was being discarded or added was of emotional, psychological or eventful significance or insignificance, or whether this would cause disruptions in the sequence of narratives. In fact contradictions were important because these would prevent the viewer from being drawn in and avoiding the significance of the structure [...]
In many ways this work reflects my scepticism of the interpretation of an artwork through the ascription of an essential meaning or depth which can be determined by reference to, amongst many other things, the artist, semiotic readings, or to questions of differing cultural 'sensibilities'. My hope is that things are a lot more uncomfortably confused.' [Kenny Macleod, notes for *The British Art Show 5*, 2000, National Touring Exhibitions, Hayward Gallery]

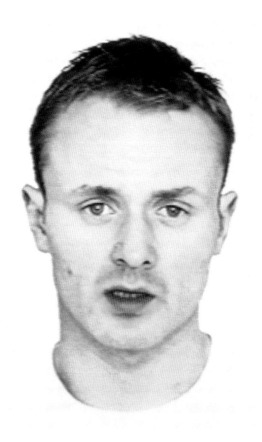

15. *The Songs of Songs*, 1999 (detail)
c-type prints; 2 parts, each 122 × 173.8 cm
Photographs by Adam Nankervis
Purchased from the artist, 2000

Born in Manila in the Philippines in 1942, David Medalla studied in Manila and New York. He went to Paris in 1960, where he participated in the city's artistic and literary scenes, before moving to London later the same year. He was Co-founder and Editor of the *Signals* review and Director of the Signals Art Gallery, London (1964-66), Founder of Exploding Galaxy, London (1967-68), Co-founder and Chairman of Artists for Democracy, London (1974) and Founder and Director of the London Biennale. Exhibitions include *Pioneers of Participation Art*, Museum of Modern Art, Oxford (1971), *Documenta 5*, Kassel, Germany (1972), *The Other Story: Afro-Asian Artists in Post-War Britain*, Hayward Gallery, London (1989) and, most recently, *Happiness*, Mori Art Museum, Tokyo (2003-04).

David Medalla's *The Songs of Songs* is a suite of photographs from performances by the artist in Spring 1999 at Madison Square Park in New York City. The photographs themselves were taken by Australian artist Adam Nankervis, with whom Medalla performed a dance drama inspired by 'The Song of Songs' from the Christian Old Testament Book of Solomon, at the MK Nightclub on Fifth Avenue in Manhattan. Although the title of these impromptus was borrowed from King Solomon, they are celebrations of world cultures. In each of the two panels the artist appears wearing different masks, which have been made from newspaper and magazine pages with holes torn out for his eyes and mouth. They include a lioness' head, a Pre-Columbian sculpture, an eagle and a bishop's mitre.

Medalla is a free spirit who has resisted assimilation by most art establishments, although his bubble machines of the 1960s have a connection with kinetic art and his work includes important interactive performance projects (such as *A Stitch in Time*, 1968-72, Arts Council Collection). During the 1980s he adopted the term 'Synoptic Realism' for his new work, which involved painting, impromptu events and photo-based pieces. Guy Brett refers to this work as 'a sophisticated kind of masquerading.' [Guy Brett, 'David Medalla' in *San Juan. The Liberal Bimonthly Magazine of Art*, 1985, Manila, p. 17] The artist himself has described his celebrations of world cultures as his 'personal ways of highlighting the fact that world cultures are polymorphic, full of mysteries and secret pleasures.' [David Medalla, 2004] IJ

David Medalla

16. *Megatripolis*, 1996
c-type print on
aluminium;
102 × 152 cm
Purchased from
The Agency, 2001

Born in London in 1971, Seamus Nicolson graduated from the Royal College of Art in 1996 and was included in the exhibition *New Contemporaries*, Camden Arts Centre, London (1997). Other group exhibitions include shows at The Agency, London (2000, 2001 and 2003) and Artopia Gallery, Milan (2004). In 2004 he will be photographing an advertising campaign for Vivienne Westwood. He lives and works in London.

Seamus Nicolson has been described as 'an ethnographer of the nocturnal inner city'. [The Agency, Press Release] *Megatripolis* was photographed as he was finishing his studies at the Royal College of Art in 1996 and is from a series shown in the 1997 exhibition *New Contemporaries* at Camden Arts Centre. Barely illuminated by a concealed flash, these London clubbers are absorbed in an ecstatic ritual. Sinister and innocent narrative may be read in this scene; for example, in the foreground a figure with 'red eye' caught by the camera lens, or the girl in a white T-shirt, who is brandishing mineral water in one hand and holding a cigarette in another. This is, literally, one of Nicolson's most obscure images. Though working with the night, he often seeks out rich arrays of detail to set against his figures. There is also generally tension between an abstract dynamic and the impression of glimpsing a story suspended. These combine in a mesmerising way in *Megatripolis*. Preferring to keep his realism as raw as possible, Nicolson resists manipulating his images beyond his initial choice of setting and timing. IJ

17. *Four Corners,
a Contest of
Opposites*, 1995
computer montage
prints on transparency
film in light-boxes;
4 parts, each
182.9 × 50.8 × 53.3,
installation
dimensions variable
Purchased from
the artist, 2000

Born in Malta in 1960, Keith Piper studied at Lanchester Polytechnic, Coventry (1979-80), Trent Polytechnic, Nottingham (1980-83) and the Royal College of Art, London (1984-86). He was a founder member of the BLK Art Group whose provocative art became evident in the touring show, *The Pan-African Connection*, which opened at London's Africa Centre in 1982. Solo shows include *Past Imperfect/ Future Tense*, The Black Art Gallery, London (1984), *A Ship Called Jesus*, Camden Arts Centre, London (1991), *Relocating the Remains*, Royal College of Art, London (1997) and *The Mechanoid's Bloodline*, Regina Gouger Miller Gallery, Pittsburg (2001). Group shows include *Boxer*, Walsall Museum and Gallery (1995), *New Histories*, Institute of Contemporary Arts, Boston (1996) and *Transferts*, Palais des Beaux-Arts de Bruxelles, Belgium. He lives and works in London.

Four Corners, a Contest of Opposites was commissioned by the Institute of International Visual Arts for the touring show *Boxer*, curated by John Gill and organised by Walsall Museum and Art Gallery. It is an installation of four upright light-boxes, illuminating life-size photographic images of the black heavyweight champions, Jack Johnson, Muhammad Ali, Joe Louis and Mike Tyson. '*A Contest of Opposites*' could suggest a stereotypical view of the good versus the bad but Piper writes in the catalogue to this exhibition with characteristic acuity about the many issues facing these men. In their day they were 'the most visible black male(s) on the planet'. Johnson and Ali were full of bravado and defiance; Louis was more conformist, allaying white fears about black fighters whereas Tyson confirmed those fears. These life stories of poverty and riches, empowerment and dis-empowerment by promoters, and adoration and vilification by the media, are charged throughout with the need to negotiate a 'racial landscape'. This work belongs to a series about sport, a supreme site for visibility of the black male body and one subject among many chosen by Piper in his redressing of black history. Piper's early work was painted swiftly and used collage but he soon began using photography and multi-media technology. IJ

Keith Piper

18. *In the House of My Father*, 1997
photographic print on aluminium;
122 × 153 cm
Purchased from the Trustees of the Estate of Donald Rodney, 1999
© The Estate of Donald Gladstone Rodney 2004

Donald Rodney was born in Birmingham in 1961. He studied at Trent Polytechnic, Nottingham (1981-85) and the Slade School of Fine Art, London (1985-87). He had solo shows at Chisenhale, London in 1990, Camerawork, London in 1991 and South London Art Gallery in 1997. He exhibited in many group exhibitions, including TSWA Four Cities project at Plymouth (1990) and *Shocks to the System*, a National Touring Exhibtion (1992-93). He died in London in 1998.

In the House of My Father is one of the final works created by Donald Rodney before his untimely death from sickle cell anaemia in 1998. It shows the artist's hand upon which sits a tiny model house, delicately constructed with fragments of Rodney's skin removed during an operation. The print was included in Rodney's last solo exhibition, *9 Night in Eldorado*, which referred to the traditional West Indian wake, where relatives and friends gather to remember the deceased over a period of nine nights. The project, dedicated to his father who had died two years earlier, served as the 'Nine Night' that at the time of his father's death Rodney had been unable to attend.

(Susan May, first published in *Here to Stay*, 1998, exhibition catalogue, Hayward Gallery Publishing, London, p. 42)

19. *Self Portraits or the Virgin Mary* from the *Self Portrait* series, 2000
c-type photograph; 3 parts, each 182.9 × 101.6 cm
Purchased from the artist, 2002

Zineb Sedira was born in Paris in 1963. She studied at Central St Martins School of Art, London (1992-95), Slade School of Art, London (1995-97) and the Royal College of Art, London (1998-2002). She has had solo exhibitions at Spacex Gallery, Exeter (2002), *Les Rencontres Internationales de la Photographie*, Arles (2002), Galleria Soggospatti, Rome (2003) and Cornerhouse, Manchester (2004); she was the initiator and a co-curator of the touring exhibition *Veil* (2003-04). She was included in the African Pavilion of the Venice Biennale in 2001. She lives and works in London.

Zineb Sedira's work draws on her experience of being a Muslim of Algerian descent educated in Paris and London. She has used photography, video and film to explore issues of cultural diversity, displacement and identity. In the triptych *Self Portraits or the Virgin Mary*, the life-sized figures are shown from different angles wearing the traditional Algerian 'haik', a full-length white veil. Sedira is interested in showing a different image of the veiled woman from the usual perception in Western art and the media where 'the veil is represented as black and oppressive and sometimes exotic'. As the title implies, she aims to ask questions and to draw attention to some of the similarities between the Catholic and Muslim faiths. The figure – the artist herself – appears like an ethereal Virgin Mary in pure white, but when she turns slightly towards the viewer she reveals a Muslim connection. AJ

Zineb Sedira

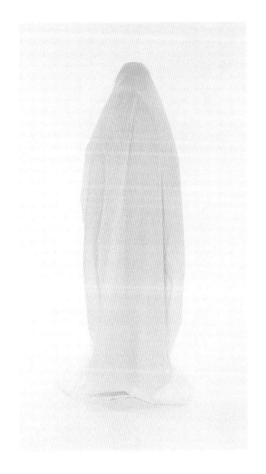

20. *Calliope* **from the** *ZABAT* **series, 1989**
cibachrome print;
152.4 × 121.9 cm
Purchased from the
artist, 1991

Maud Sulter was born in Glasgow in 1960. She graduated from the University of Derby in 1990. Solo exhibitions include *Hysteria*, Tate Gallery, Liverpool (1991) and *Syrcas*, Wrexham Arts Centre and tour (1994-95). Recent group shows include *Narcissus*, and *The Fine Art of Photography*, Scottish National Portrait Gallery, Edinburgh (2001) and *Encontros da Imagen*, Braga, Portugal (2002). She has a recently published monograph *Jeanne: A Melodrama* (National Galleries of Scotland, 2003). She was the British representative at the 1st Johannesburg Biennial in 1995. Sulter is also a poet and writer and has curated many exhibitions. While continuing to produce lens-based work, she has moved into screenwriting and currently divides her time between Preston, Los Angeles and a farmhouse on the Scottish borders.

Calliope is one of a series of nine gilt-framed portraits of black women, each dressed with appropriate attributes to represent one of the Muses. As black women they challenge the idea of the Muses as part of 'white' European culture as well as celebrating black women's creativity. In texts that accompany each image the Muses are given the power of speech and their histories reveal the misrepresentation of black history. As the Muse of Epic Poetry, the sitter for *Calliope*, who is Maud Sulter herself, assumes a pose reminiscent of a nineteenth-century portrait and on the table before her is a framed photograph. One of her roles is to signify representation itself, but she also represents Jeanne Duval, the so-called 'Black Venus', who was Charles Baudelaire's mistress and the inspiration for his poem 'Les fleurs du mal', although her contribution has never been properly acknowledged. IJ

(First published in *Shocks to the System*, 1991, exhibition catalogue, National Touring Exhibitions, South Bank Centre, London, p. 70)

21. *Oi!*, 1998
r-type photograph;
3 parts,
each 244 × 197 cm
Purchased from
White Cube, 1999

Gavin Turk was born in Guildford in 1967. He studied at the Chelsea School of Art (1986-89) and Royal College of Art, London (1989-91). He has had solo exhibitions at South London Art Gallery (1998), Centre d'art contemporain, Geneva (2000), New Art Gallery, Walsall (2002) and the New Art Centre Sculpture Park and Gallery, Salisbury (2003), as well as regular showings at White Cube, London. He lives and works in London.

By layering references to seminal works of art in his own photographs, sculptures and paintings, Turk has challenged and teased questions of reputation, authenticity and authorship in art. He himself has taken the lead role in several works, appearing as Sid Vicious and Jacques-Louis David's martyred Marat. In the triptych *Oi!* Turk is dressed as a tramp. Bleary-eyed and in filthy clothing, he points a finger in what could be seen as an aggressive gesture if it were not for the fact that he is obviously too inebriated to be capable of any extreme action. This pose also mirrors his sculpture of Sid Vicious shooting from the hip, which in turn echoes Andy Warhol's 1963 cowboy portrait of Elvis Presley. In the same year as *Oi!*, Turk also made a life-sized waxwork version of the same tramp, *Bum*. Both works were the result of Turk's performance as a drunkard at the private view of the now famous *Sensation* exhibition at the Royal Academy in 1997. AJ

Gavin Turk

22. *Note*, **1992**
c-type photograph
on aluminium;
180 × 122 cm
Purchased from the
artists, 1995

Jane and Louise Wilson

Jane and Louise Wilson are twins and were born in Newcastle in 1967. They studied at Newcastle Polytechnic (1986-89) and Duncan of Jordanstone College of Art, Dundee (1986-89) respectively and then together at Goldsmiths College, London (1990-92). They have had solo exhibitions at the Serpentine Gallery, London (1999) and Kunstwerke, Berlin (2002), as well as regular exhibitions at the Lisson Gallery, London. They were awarded a DAAD scholarship to Berlin in 1996 and were short-listed for the Turner Prize in 1999. They live and work in London.

Jane and Louise Wilson have collaborated as artists since 1988. They say, 'our lives are interchangeable and we live in chaos', but in fact the circumstances of their work are carefully organised. *Note* is the first in a series of photographs constructed in their flat, and was sparked off by a real event when someone had tried to smash down their front door and two weeks after sent a note of apology. Curious to see their home through the eyes of a stranger, they used the note as a starting point for life-size images in which recognition and estrangement co-exist. The photographs are placed in the gallery at heights and angles corresponding to the positions from which they were taken.

(Helen Luckett, first published in *Here to Stay*, 1998, exhibition catalogue, Hayward Gallery Publishing, London, p. 54)

Further reading

Neal Ascherson, *Shocks to the System. Social and political issues in recent British art from the Arts Council Collection*, 1991, exhibition catalogue, South Bank Centre, London

David A. Bailey, Gilane Tawadros (eds), *Veil: Veiling, Representation and Contemporary Art*, 2003, exhibition catalogue, InIVA, London

Neal Brown, Sarah Kent, Matthew Collings, *Tracey Emin*, 1998, Jay Jopling, London

Virginia Button, Charles Esche, *Intelligence*, 2000, exhibition catalogue, Tate, London

Virginia Button, *The Turner Prize. Twenty Years*, 2003, exhibition catalogue, Tate, London

Christopher Coppock and Malcolm Dickson, *Death's Dance Floor*, 1998, exhibition catalogue, Ffotogallery and Streetlevel, Cardiff

Lisa Corrin, *Jane and Louise Wilson*, 1999, exhibition catalogue, Serpentine Gallery, London

Sean Cubitt, Claire Doherty, *Alan Currall*, 2004, exhibition catalogue, Film and Video Umbrella, Stoke-on-Trent

David Deitcher, David Frankel, Amanda Cruz, Isaac Julien, *The Film Art of Isaac Julien*, 2000, part catalogue and part collection writing, Center for Curatorial Studies, Bard College, New York

Alex Farquharson, *Gavin Turk*, 1998, exhibition catalogue, Jay Jopling/South London Gallery, London

Sunil Gupta, *Pictures from Here. Sunil Gupta*, 2003, Autograph/Chris Boot, London

Lubaina Himid, *Syrcas. Maud Sulter*, 1993, exhibition catalogue, Wrexham Library Arts Centre

Richard Hylton, Eddie Chambers, Virginia Nimarkoh, *Donald Rodney*, 2003, Autograph, London

Isobel Johnstone, *The Saatchi Gift to the Arts Council Collection*, 2000, exhibition catalogue, Hayward Gallery, London

Susan May, *Here to Stay: Arts Council Collection Purchases of the 1990s*, 1998, exhibition catalogue, Hayward Gallery, London

Kobena Mercer, *Keith Piper*, 1997, exhibition catalogue, InIVA, London

Jeremy Millar, *Graham Gussin*, 2002, exhibition catalogue, Ikon Gallery, Birmingham

Bisi Silva and Richard Hylton, *Heads of State*, 1998, Fourth Dial Art Publications, London

Michael Tarantino, *Richard Billingham*, 2000, exhibition catalogue, Ikon Gallery, Birmingham

Marcus Verhagen, Gilane Tawadros, *Recent Sonia Boyce: La La La*, 2001, exhibition catalogue, Douglas F. Cooley Memorial Art Gallery, Portland